Developing World Class Products

Techniques For Product Managers To Better Understand What Their Customers Really Want

"Practical, proven examples of how to get the customer insights that are necessary in order to have a successful product"

Dr. Jim Anderson

Published by:
Blue Elephant Consulting
Tampa, Florida

Copyright © 2017 by Dr. Jim Anderson

All rights reserved. No part of this book may be reproduced of transmitted in any form or by any means, electronic or mechanical, including photocopying, recording or by any information storage and retrieval system without written permission of the publisher, except for inclusion of brief quotations in a review.

Printed in the United States of America

Library of Congress Control Number: 2017919213

ISBN-13: 978-1987795370
ISBN-10: 1987795377

Warning – Disclaimer

The purpose of this book is to educate and entertain. This book does not promise or guarantee that anyone following the ideas, tips, suggestions, techniques or strategies will be successful. The author, publisher and distributor(s) shall have neither liability nor responsibility to anyone with respect to any loss or damage caused, or alleged to be caused, directly or indirectly by the information contained in this book.

Recent Books By The Author

Product Management

- Managing Your Product Manager Career: How Product Managers Can Find And Succeed In The Right Job

- How Product Managers Can Sell More Of Their Product: Tips & Techniques For Product Managers To Better Understand How To Sell Their Product

Public Speaking

- Creating Speeches That Work: How To Create A Speech That Will Make Your Message Be Remembered Forever!

- How To Organize A Speech In Order To Make Your Point: How to put together a speech that will capture and hold your audience's attention

CIO Skills

- How CIOs Can Bring Business And IT Together: How CIOs Can Use Their Technical Skills To Help Their Company Solve Real-World Business Problems

- New IT Technology Issues Facing CIOs: How CIOs Can Stay On Top Of The Changes In The Technology That

Powers The Company

IT Manager Skills

- How IT Managers Can Use New Technology To Meet Today's IT Challenges: Technologies That IT Managers Can Use In Order to Make Their Teams More Productive

- How To Build High Performance IT Teams: Tips And Techniques That IT Managers Can Use In Order To Develop Productive Teams

Negotiating

- The Art Of Packaging A Negotiation: How To Develop The Skill Of Assembling Potential Trades In Order To Get The Best Possible Outcome

- Getting What You Want In A Negotiation By Learning How To Signal: How To Develop The Skill Of Effective Signaling In A Negotiation In Order To Get The Best Possible Outcome

Miscellaneous

- How To Heal A Broken Leg – Fast!: Understanding how to deal with a broken leg in order to start walking again quickly

- How Software Defined Networking (SDN) Is Going To Change Your World Forever: The Revolution In Network Design And How It Affects

Note: See a complete list of books by Dr. Jim Anderson at the back of this book.

Acknowledgements

Any book like this one is the result of years of real-world work experience. In my over 25 years of working for 7 different firms, I have met countless fantastic people and I've been mentored by some truly exceptional ones. Although I've probably forgotten some of the people who made me the person that I am today, here is my attempt to finally give them the recognition that they so truly deserve:

- Thomas P. Anderson
- Art Puett
- Bobbi Marshall
- Bob Boggs

Dr. Jim Anderson

This book is dedicated to my wife Lori. None of this would have been possible without her love and support.

Thanks for the best years of my life (so far)...!

Table Of Contents

MANAGING YOUR CUSTOMERS IS PART OF A PRODUCT MANAGER'S JOB 9

ABOUT THE AUTHOR 11

CHAPTER 1: PRODUCT MANAGERS NEED TO KNOW WHAT THEIR COMPANY'S COST OF CAPITAL IS 16

CHAPTER 2: HOW PRODUCT MANAGERS CAN MANAGE THE AGE GAP ON THEIR PRODUCT TEAMS 21

CHAPTER 3: HOW SHOULD A PRODUCT MANAGER HANDLE PRODUCT TEAM CONFLICTS? 25

CHAPTER 4: WHY PRODUCT MANAGERS NEED CHECKLISTS IN ORDER TO BE SUCCESSFUL 29

CHAPTER 5: HOW TO CREATE A PRODUCT TIMELINE THAT WORKS . 33

CHAPTER 6: THE SECRET TO CREATING A CUSTOMER-FACING PRODUCT ROADMAP 38

CHAPTER 7: WHAT CAN PRODUCT MANAGERS LEARN FROM HOW THE IPHONE WAS BORN? 43

CHAPTER 8: APPLYING DIGITAL PRODUCT MANAGEMENT TO PERFUME 47

CHAPTER 9: WHAT CAN ESPN TEACH YOU ABOUT GROWING YOUR PRODUCT? 51

CHAPTER 10: WHAT DOES THE INTERNET OF THINGS MEAN TO PRODUCT MANAGERS? 55

CHAPTER 11: IS TWITTER OUT OF CONTROL? 59

CHAPTER 12: AMAZON PLANS ON GETTING INTO THE GROCERY BUSINESS 63

Managing Your Customers Is Part Of A Product Manager's Job

As product managers, we are the ones who are in charge of developing a product that our customers are going to want and our competitors are going to fear. There is no one right way to develop a winning product, rather there is a particular set of skills that every product manager has to develop in order to create products that will be successful.

It all starts with understanding just exactly how much a product is going to cost to create. Cost of capital is a term that the business side of the house uses to talk about such things and product managers need to understand what it means and how to use it. The teams that we'll assemble to create our products will be diverse in many different ways. One way will be age. This means that a product manager is going to have to get good at finding ways to have different age workers all get along with each other. When you start to understand all of the different things that a product manager has to do at the same time in order to develop a product, you'll start to understand why checklists are a product manager's best friend.

Developing a product means that the product manager is going to have to know when the product will be ready to be sold. This means that a timeline for the product will have to be both developed and then adhered to. Just creating a product is not the end of the story. There will be more versions that will have more functionality. This means that a product manager will have to develop a roadmap and share with both the development team and existing and potential customers. As we enter the age of digital product management, product managers need to know that they don't have to solve all problems by themselves. They can look at other successful products, such as the iPhone, for tips and hints at how to develop products that will be successful.

In some markets a single product starts to dominate that market. As product managers we'd all like to emulate this success and that's why it's important that we study brands such as ESPN in order to understand how they have been able to achieve the success that they have had. Change is a constant part of what it means to be a product manager and the arrival of the internet of things promises to change everything. This means that we need to understand what it is and how it will impact us. Communicating with our customers is a key part of being a product manager and the Twitter micro blogging service has become an important tool. However, as it continues to evolve we need to look closely at it to see if it is still useful for us. Entering new markets is how product managers can ensure that their products continue to grow. Amazon's recent entry into the grocery business can show us how to accomplish this.

For more information on what it takes to be a great product manager, check out my blog, The Accidental Product Manager, at:

www.TheAccidentalPM.com

Good luck!

- Dr. Jim Anderson

About The Author

I must confess that I never set out to be a product manager. When I went to school, I studied Computer Science and thought that I'd get a nice job programming and that would be that. Well, at least part of that plan worked out!

My first job was working for Boeing on their F/A-18 fighter jet program. I spent my days programming fighter jet software in assembly language and I loved it. The U.S. government decided to save some money and went looking for other countries to sell this plane to. This put me into an unfamiliar role: I started to meet with foreign military officials in order to explain what my product did.

Time moved on and so did I. I found myself working for Siemens, the big German telecommunications company. They were making phone switches and selling them to the seven U.S. phone companies. The problem was that the switches were too complicated. Customers couldn't tell the difference between one complicated phone switch from another complicated phone switch.

The Siemens sales folks were in a bind. They didn't know enough about how the switches worked to tell their customers why they should buy them. Siemens reached out into their engineering unit looking for anyone who could help the sales teams out. I put my hand up and overnight I became a product manager.

Since then I've spent over 20 years working as a product manager for both big companies and startups. This has given me an opportunity to do everything that a product manager does many, many times. I know what works as well as what doesn't work.

I now live in Tampa Florida where I spend my time managing my consulting business, Blue Elephant Consulting, teaching college courses at the Florida Polytechnic University, and traveling to work with companies like yours to share the knowledge that I have about how product managers can make their product be a success.

I'm always available to answer questions and I can be reached at:

Dr. Jim Anderson
Blue Elephant Consulting
Email: jim@BlueElephantConsulting.com
Facebook: http://goo.gl/1TVoK
Web: **www.BlueElephantConsulting.com**

"Unforgettable communication skills that will set your ideas free..."

Create Products Your Customers Want At A Price That They Are Willing To Pay!

Dr. Jim Anderson is available to provide training and coaching on the two topics that are the most important to product managers everywhere: how do I create the products that my customers want and what should I price them at?

Dr. Anderson believes that in order to both learn and remember what he says, product managers need to laugh. Each one of his speeches is full of fun and humor so that what he says "sticks" with everyone.

Dr. Anderson's Product Management Training Includes:

1. How can you segment your market?
2. What problems are your customers having right now?
3. Which of your customer's problems does your product solve?
4. How much of this problem does your product solve?
5. How much will it cost your customer if they don't fix this problem?

Dr. Jim Anderson presents over 100 speeches per year. To invite Dr. Anderson to speak at your event, contact him at:

Phone: 813-418-6970 or
Email: jim@BlueElephantConsulting.com

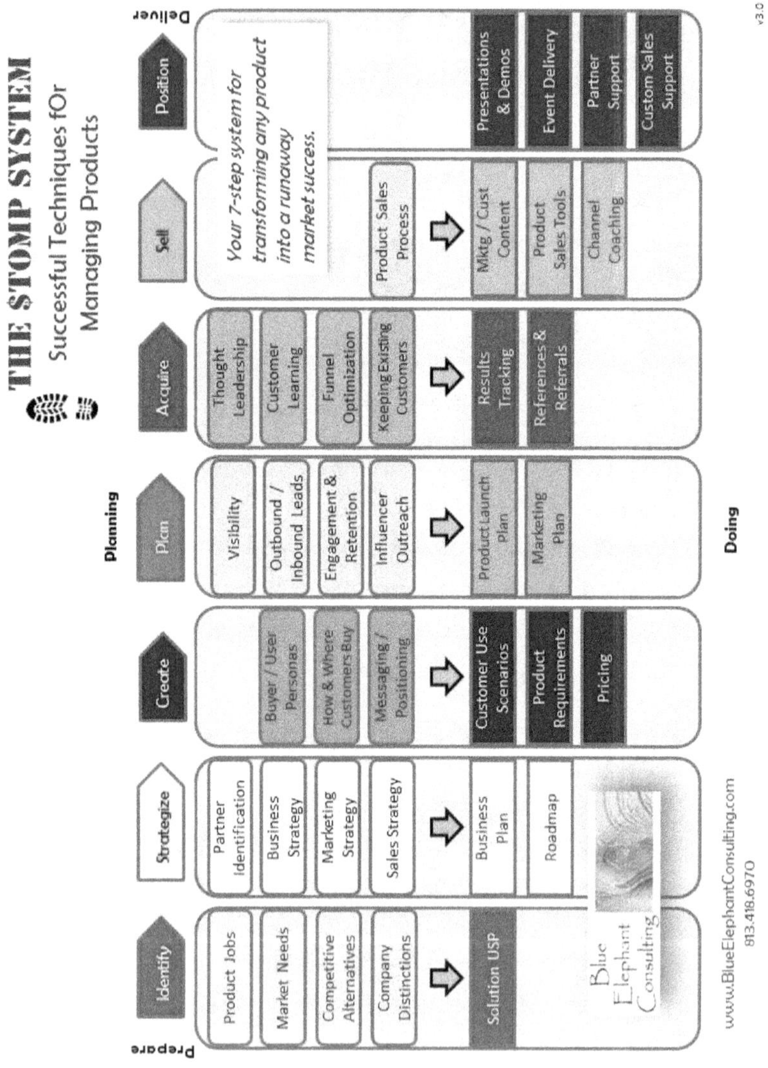

The **$TOMP** product management system has been created by **Blue Elephant Consulting** to help product managers know what to do and when to do it in order for a product to be successful.

14

Chapter 1

Product Managers Need To Know What Their Company's Cost Of Capital Is

Chapter 1: Product Managers Need To Know What Their Company's Cost Of Capital Is

You've just been put in charge of managing the best product ever. Based on the product development definition, you know that this product is going to be a run-away success: it solves a critical problem that a lot of customers are currently facing. There's just one problem: either the product does not yet exist or it exists, but doesn't do what it needs to do. **You're going to need some money** – what's it going to take to get your company to fund your product?

What Is The "Cost Of Capital"?

One of the things that too many product managers forget is that **their company does not HAVE to fund their product**. Yes, we can get all caught up in the fantastic market potential of our product, but from the company's perspective there are a lot of other things that they can do with their money.

What this means is that when you go asking for the funding that you are going to need in order to make your product successful, you are going to have to convince some people that your product represents **the best place for the company to spend its money**. This means that you're going to have to have a talk about the cost of capital. Figure this one out and you'll have something else to add to your product manager resume.

Generally speaking, the company's finance department is going to be in charge of **running the numbers on your request for funding**. What we product managers don't often realize is that the company many not have the money that we're requesting just sitting around. Instead, in order to fund our product, the company may need to dip into both its cash reserves (equity) as well as going out and borrowing some money.

Exactly how they go about doing this is something that too many product managers take a hands-off approach to. I'm going to suggest that we spend a little time talking about what you need to know about your cost of capital so that you've got the best chance of **getting the funding that you want**.

Assumptions Your Company Makes About Their Cost Of Capital

The world of finance can be mysterious to many product managers. However, with a little investigation you can quickly learn enough to be able to have a good discussion with your colleagues in the finance department. Here are **6 assumptions** that your finance team may be making about how much the capital for your project is going to cost the company:

1. **Investment Time Horizon:** We all know what this one is: how long after they give you the money is your product going to start to make money for the company? All too often a finance department has one value that they use for this (1 year, 5 years, etc.). However, the investment time horizon should vary according to your product: innovative products will take longer to generate a profit than line extensions.

2. **How Much Does Debt Cost?:** When the folks in finance are trying to determine how much it's going to cost the company to borrow the money that they'll spend on your product, they need to find a benchmark to use. All too often a finance department will use the current average rate on outstanding debt. This is the wrong way to do it. They really need to be using the forecasted rate on new debt issuance. Make sure that they're doing it the right way!

3. **The Risk-Free Rate:** When trying to determine how much of a return your product should generate, finance people generally start by trying to determine how much of a return an investor would want to get from a risk-free investment. What this means is that they take a look at how much the U.S. Treasury is paying on investments. However, this is where the problem can pop up: which U.S. Treasury rate will they be looking at: the 10-year rate, the 5-year rate, or the 30-year bond? Make sure that when your request for funding gets compared to other requests, that apples-to-apples risk-free rate rates are being used.

4. **Equity Market Premium:** Because investing in any project is risky, your finance department will be determining a risk premium for the funding that you are requesting. Many companies use a number between 5%-6%. However, this is probably an old number that hasn't been changed in a long time. Take a look and see if you think that it should go down. If so, have a talk with your finance department.

5. **Beta:** The volatility of your company's stock plays a role in how much equity is going cost. A beta that is greater than 1 means that the company has greater-than-average volatility. A beta less than 1 means that your company has less-than-average volatility. Where a product manager may run into problems is when your finance department can't agree on what time frame to measure the company's volatility over: 1 year, 2 years, 3 years, or 5 years?

6. **Debt-To-Equity Ratio:** It turns out that your product may be financed by a mixture of cash that the company has (equity) and debt. How much of each to use is something that the finance department needs to determine. The problem is that they often can't decide

if they should base this decision on the company's current book debt, targeted book debt, or current market debt. Picking the wrong one can drive your cost of capital way up.

7. **Risk Of The Product:** The final factor in determining the cost of capital for your product is to come up with an overall risk factor for your product. If the company takes a look at another product with a comparable level of risk, then they are doing it correctly. However, if they just tack on a percentage point to the value that they've already calculated for your cost of capital then they are doing it wrong. Find out how your finance team is coming up with this number!

What All Of This Means For You

The next time that you are handed a product to manage, you need to review your product manager job description and take a careful look at what you are being given. There are probably some changes that need to be made to your product in order for it to truly be successful. This means that **you are going to need to get some company funding**.

In order to get the funding that you need, you're going to have to work with the company's finance department. **They'll be using the company's cost of capital to make funding decisions about your product**. This means that you are going to have to use the 6 techniques that we've discussed to make sure that they are using the correct cost of capital.

The world of finance can appear to be strange and intimidating to an uneducated product manager. That's why you need to learn about the cost of capital and then sit down and talk with your finance department in order to **ensure that you're going to get the best deal possible** for your product. If you are going to be a successful product manager, then you're going to have to know how to speak the language of finance.

Chapter 2

How Product Managers Can Manage The Age Gap On Their Product Teams

Chapter 2: How Product Managers Can Manage The Age Gap On Their Product Teams

Product managers often don't manage any direct reports. However, in order to have a successful product, we always seem to find ourselves **in charge of a sort of "virtual team" of people** who are sprinkled throughout the company. It turns out that in order for our product to be a success, we need to do a good job of managing this virtual team. That means that we've got to find a way to deal with the age gap issue…

Where Did The Age Gap Come From?

Once you get done creating your product development definition, it's time to manage the workers who make up your product's virtual team. This won't always be the case, but for right now **we've got three different generations of workers that make up our teams**. First off, there are the so called "Baby Boomers" who were born 1946-1964 – these are the older members of your team. Next comes the "Generation X" workers who were born between 1964 – 1980. Finally you have the newest set of workers who are called the Millennials and they were born between 1980-2000. Good luck getting all of them to work together to make your product a success!

The big problem for a product manager is that each one of these groups likes to **communicate in a different way** and they all respond to different types of motivations. Clearly, there is not one solution that is going to get them all on board when it comes to your product. If you can come up with a solution to this problem, then you'll have something to add to your product manager resume.

How Should Product Managers Handle The Age Gap

The first issue that you are going to have to deal with as a product manager is uncovering **how each generational group wants to be communicated with**. The answer is going to depend on what communication tools they grew up with and are most comfortable using. The Baby Boomers like using both the telephone and face-to-face communication. The Gen X workers are more comfortable using email and instant messaging. Finally, the Millennials prefer to use their smart phones and communicate using social media applications such as Facebook and Twitter.

What each generation **wants to get out of their job** (and working on your product) will differ also. The older members of your virtual product team will have more work experience in more traditional hierarchical organizations. The younger members will be more familiar with flatter organizations where they believe that they can contribute and that their voices will be heard. Note that this can lead to clashes where your older workers believe that the right to be heard has to be earned over time.

As a product manager it's going to be your responsibility to **discover how each member of your product's virtual team wants to communicate** and what they want to get out of working on your product. This means that the burden of discovering this information is on you to find out. Once you have this information you can start to tailor how you communicate with the rest of the team in order to make sure that your message and your requests are being received and understood by the people that you need to take action.

What Does All Of This Mean For You

It would be a perfect world if everyone that worked on your product's "virtual team" was exactly the same. However, the world is not perfect and you've got three different generations of workers to deal with on your team even if that was never a part of your product manager job description.

The Baby Boomers, Generation X, and Millennials all have different ways of communicating. Additionally, they are looking to get different things out of their jobs. As product manager you need to discover what these things are and then use them to connect with the members of your team.

It's not going to be easy and there may be people who belong to one generation who like to do things the way that another generation does not. That's ok. You need to take the time to find out how your product's team wants to interact with you and then you need to use that information. Keep in mind that your product is only going to be as successful as the team that works on it is. Learn what they want, give it to them, and watch them work to make your product a success.

Chapter 3

How Should A Product Manager Handle Product Team Conflicts?

Chapter 3: How Should A Product Manager Handle Product Team Conflicts?

I'm currently in charge of a team of skilled product development professionals who spend their time helping me to refine my product development definition. They each have their own set of skills that they bring to my product and I need each of them to be operating at peak efficiency if I want to have any hope of my product being a success. However, I'm currently facing a big problem: **two members of my team flat out don't get along with each other**. What's a product manager to do?

How The Problem Started

How does any problem between team members start? In all honesty, I'm not quite sure. I believe that this problem existed long before I took over control of this team. Both parties involved are actually very nice people and they seem to get along with everyone else. **They just don't like each other**.

The first signs of a problem showed up when I started to be **copied on a series of emails exchanged between these two**. What they were talking about was a series of changes that needed to be made to some product related documents. The question seemed to revolve around who had the right to tell who to do what.

I'm willing to admit that I probably **missed an important warning marker here** – I saw the emails but I didn't realize the issue that was only now starting to surface. Yes, I should have jumped right in and tried to resolve this issue from the start; however, I just saw it as an email exchange between two team members – the fact that I had been CC'ed should have been my first clue that all was not good. I need to find a way to solve this problem and if I can, then I'll have something to add to my product manager resume.

What My Options Are

As you can well imagine, **things went from bad to worst**. I started to get calls from the people involved in this workplace feud telling me about how the other party had somehow wronged them. The issues that they brought up ranged from the possibly legit issue of who had ultimate control over a given document to the ridicules issue of someone not saying "hello" to them when they come into the office in the morning.

My big challenge here was **how was I going to resolve this issue**. One of the parties involved said something that really struck home with me: "...we'll never be friends" When she said this, I realized that my job was not to get them to be friends, but rather to find a way so that they could work together as colleagues. This was a big breakthrough for me – as an engineer, I'm always looking for the "perfect" solution and I probably would never have been able to find one in this situation.

I've taken all of what you would probably call **the standard steps** to defuse this situation: I've talked with both parties, I've told them that they need to pull it together for the betterment of the company, I've divided the work up and assigned clear owners to the different parts. However, ill will continues to exist.

My work here is not done. One option that I'm considering is making the repair of the relationship **an objective** for each of the team members. You know, something that they'll be evaluated on at the end of the year. This would take the issue out of my hands and put it right where it belongs – in their hands. I'm not yet sure if this would be a powerful management technique or simply a case of passing the buck. In real life there are no neat solutions to messy management problems.

What All Of This Means For You

As product managers, what we'd like to be able to spend our time doing is focusing on our product and finding ways for it to be more successful. However, what we need to realize that that we're not going to be able to do this if our team is not working as a seamless unit. When there's conflict within our team, **we need to take action** no matter if this is in your product manager job description or not.

I'm currently facing a situation where **two of the members of my team don't get along**. I'm getting calls and emails where one complains about what the other has done to them. It is now my job to step in and fix this problem. A key point to remember is that both parties are both at fault and they are both going to have to change in order to fix the problem.

Yes, these kinds of personality based conflicts can be a distraction from what a product manager really needs to be spending his or her time on. However, they are real and **they do need to be resolved**. Allowing team problems to fester will just keep the team from being as successful as it can be. As a product manager you need to step into the situation and use your diplomacy skills to move both parties through the conflict and onto higher ground. No, it's not going to be easy, but it is going to be necessary.

Chapter 4

4 Ways Product Managers Can Let Why Product Managers Need Checklists In Order To Be Successful

Chapter 4: Why Product Managers Need Checklists In Order To Be Successful

Let's face it, being a product manager means that there are **a lot of different things** that you are responsible for accomplishing. Many of these things are very small details, a few are medium sized tasks, and just a couple may be very large. However, if you "drop the ball" on any of the things that have to be done you may put the success of your product at risk. How can a product manager become perfect and never forget to do everything that has to be done?

The Power Of Checklists

Let's spend just a moment thinking about **all of the different things that a product manager does**: collects requirements, creates a product development definition, creates a roadmap, oversees product development, creates collateral, works trade shows, meets with press, trains sales, etc. Each one of these tasks has a long list of subtasks associated with it that all need to be accomplished.

I can only speak for myself, but there is no way that I can ever remember everything that I have to do. It gets even harder when you realize that **a product manager is always multitasking** – we'll work on one thing for a while and then we'll have to switch to another task before we can come back and work on what we were working on once again. It's pretty easy to see how things can start to fall through the cracks. Forgetting things is not something that will look good on your product manager resume.

This is exactly the type of problem that a checklist is designed to solve. By taking the time before you start a project to write down all of the individual tasks that you'll have to perform in order for the project to be successful, **you'll have a master list**

of what needs to be done. As you accomplish the varied tasks, you can check them off your list. You'll always know how much more work you have to do and you'll know when you have finally completed the project.

How To Use Checklists To Be A Better Product Manager

Now this may all sound great for you; however, how can a product manager use a checklist in the real world. Well, I've got some great news for you: I've just completed a project where **checklists stepped in and saved my life**.

I had created a series of books about my product that I had self-published though Amazon. This had been very successful and my books were now appearing on Amazon's bookshelves and were being bought. However, I soon discovered that my books **were not available** via iTunes or available to be purchased at Barns & Nobel. I had to do something to solve this problem.

The answer was to upload electronic copies of my books to a service called Smashwords. **They would then sell my books through these additional channels.** My problem was that each one of my ebooks had to be edited and changed in order to meet the Smashwords book format. In fact it turned out that 30 different edits needed to be made to each one of my books. There was no way that I was ever going to be able to remember to make all of these edits.

I solved this problem by going through my first book and discovering what edits had to be made. Each time I submitted the book to Smashwords it would be rejected and they would tell me why. I would make a change and document it in a list that I was creating in an Excel spreadsheet. By the time Smashwords finally accepted my ebook, **I had a list that contained 30 different steps.** From then on it was a simple process to use that checklist to convert my other books to the proper format. I never had Smashwords reject another one of my ebooks and I was able to accomplish my conversion project in under a week!

What All Of This Means For You

Product managers know that **success lies in the details of the job**. Each one of the tasks that we have to do has a million small tasks associated with it. We need to successfully accomplish these tasks in order to be a successful product manager. This really should be part of every product manager job description.

Since there is no way that we can possibly ever remember everything that we have to do, **we need to learn to use checklists**. By taking the time to create a checklist we are able to identify everything that we're going to have to do. Using a checklist also allows us to determine how far along we are in a task and we can determine when we are finally done.

Checklists are part of how product managers are successful. Take the time to create good checklists once and they will serve you each time you have to accomplish a task. Everyone will be very impressed with **your attention to detail**; however, you'll be the only one who knows what your secret is!

Chapter 5

How To Create A Product Timeline That Works

Chapter 5: How To Create A Product Timeline That Works

Ah, product timelines. This is arguably one of the most visible and one of the most difficult things that a product manager is called on to create in order to communicate your product development definition. It turns out that creating a timeline is not really all that hard to do. However, **creating a timeline that is both accurate and useful to other people is quite hard to do**. I recently had to help a startup company create their very first product timeline and it reminded me just how tricky this task can be…

What A Timeline Needs To Be Able To Do

Before you go to all of the time and effort that creating a timeline requires, perhaps you should first make sure that you understand just exactly why you'll be creating timeline in the first place. **A timeline is nothing more than a communication tool**. As a product manager you want to be able to let everyone who comes into contact with your product know what the product is going to be able to do and when it is going to be able to do it. This is the kind of thing that should be on everyone's product manager resume

Just as important as knowing what a timeline is, is **knowing what it is not**. The first thing that we need to realize is that a timeline is not set in concrete. Just because you create a timeline today does not mean that things are going to work out this way. Rather, you should view a timeline for what it really is: your best guess at what's going to happen in the future. If things change, then you'll go back and change your timeline to reflect the new reality of the world.

A timeline is not how you communicate with your customer what your product will do in the future. Perhaps I should say this a little differently; the timeline that you create to communicate within the company will be different from the timeline that you use to talk to customers. Your internal timeline will contain more details than any document that you create to talk with customers about where your product is going. Customers don't need to know about all of those details and when things change, you'd have a lot more explaining to do if you shared too much.

How I Created A Timeline That Actually Works

The company that I was brought in to work with already had a fairly successful product. They wanted to prepare for the future and they knew the informal verbal communication system that they had been using to talk about what features would be going into the product would no longer work. **What they needed was a timeline** that could be used throughout the company to make sure that everyone knew what was coming and when it was coming.

The process that I went through in order to create a timeline for them had four separate steps to it:

Step 1: Work with development to identify all possible changes

Everyone pretty much knew the changes that had to be made to the product going forward. Some were written down, some were not. I sat down with the development team and we went through each and every possible new feature without judging its value. For each feature I captured a name, a description, a source, an effort estimate, and who would actually do the work. In the end I had a list of 145 features.

Step 2: Work with business to identify priorities

My next step was to sit down with the business side of the house and have them prioritize each of the 145 identified features. I had them use a 1-10 scale where 10 was the most valuable and 1 was the least valuable. This was very painful for everyone involved to do, but we toughed it out and eventually made it to the end of the list.

Step 3: Work with business to identify priorities within priorities
Sadly, the next step involved the same set of business partners once again. This time around I had them sit down and with the priority 10 features (the most important), I had them rank them from 1-25 (there were 25 priority 10 features). I then had them do the same thing for the priority 9 and priority 8 features. I didn't worry about anything less than that because I figured that things will change before we get to them.

Step 4: Create a timeline
The final step. Now that I knew all of the features, what their priority was, how long it would take to implement the feature, and who would do the work, it was fairly easy to create a timeline starting with the high priority features and working towards the lower priority features. One additional step that I did was to color code each of the planned features. The product had 16 major functions and I assigned a color to each function so that I could see which functions would be getting new features. What I discovered was that most of the changes that we would be working on were internal – no customer would ever see them, they would just make the product work faster / better.

What All Of This Means For You

A product timeline is **a critical communication tool** that product managers use to let the rest of the company know what their product will be able to do and when it will be able to do it. Creating one of these should be a part of everyone's product manager job description. The challenge that we run into when we are creating a timeline is that if we don't do it correctly, then nobody will bother to use it and we'll have just ended up wasting our time.

When we create a product timeline, **we need to be careful to use it correctly**. Timelines are fluid things that probably will change over time. They are not the right way to communicate with your customer what new features are planned for your product. Instead, you need to work with both the development and business sides of your company to create a prioritized list of what features need to be added to your product.

If you can get this product timeline creation thing done correctly, then you'll discover that everything having to do with your product just seems to move along that much easier. Once everyone **knows what "the plan" is for your product**, they'll be able to better arrange their schedules to support you. Learn from how I created my product timeline and create one that works for your product!

Chapter 6

The Secret To Creating A Customer-Facing Product Roadmap

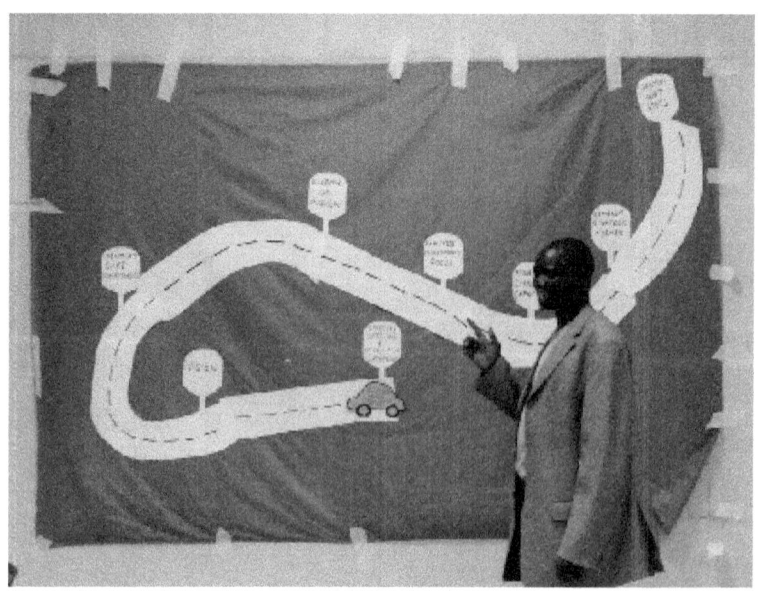

Chapter 6: The Secret To Creating A Customer-Facing Product Roadmap

I like having customers. You like having customers. In fact, once we get a customer we sure would like to hang on to them. The problem is that our customers always want our products to do more, more, more for them. What this means is that **we always need to be adding new features and capabilities to our products**. Where things can get a bit tricky is when it comes to just exactly how we tell our existing and prospective customers about what new features are coming and when they will arrive.

What Kind Of Information Goes Into A Customer Facing Roadmap?

Let's face it – creating a customer facing roadmap is a tricky balancing act. The reason that this is such a challenging thing to do is because **you want to provide your existing and potential customers with just enough information, but not too much**. Just to make things a little bit more complicated, product managers always have to assume that their customer facing roadmaps will eventually fall into their competition's hands. You never want to provide them with too much information…

So now we come down to the key question: what to include? Knowing the answer to this question will be something that you can put on your product manager resume. The first thing that we need to agree on is **what do customers really want to know?** They want to know when new functionality will be added to the product – this will allow them to create internal plans to start to use that functionality. They don't need to have all of the details about the new functions, but they do need to have enough in order to understand what they will be getting.

The other thing that a customer facing roadmap has to clearly communicate is **when your customer is going to be getting the features that you have promised them?** Once again we are venturing into a minefield here. If you tell your customer that they'll have a new function on April 28th of this year, they will be expecting to have the function on that date. If you have a development slip, a parts problem, etc. and your schedule slips, then you will end up disappointing your customer. You need to come up with a way to communicate the information without exposing yourself to letting your customer down.

What Is The Best Way To Present A Customer Facing Roadmap?

Ok, so now we know what needs to go into a customer facing roadmap. Now let's talk about how best to put it there. The first step is going to be to **come up with a timeline for your roadmap**. Next you are going to want to lay in a description of the functionality that you'll be providing at each point in time on your roadmap. Finally, you'll want to wrap the entire roadmap in a wrapper that clearly communicates the timeframe that it is valid for.

The timeline that you use for your customer facing roadmap may be the most important decision that you make. Let us agree that **providing too much detail when it comes to when your features will be delivered is a mistake**. This means that you need to stay away from specific dates. I'm going to take this up one step further, you are going to want to stay away from specific months – it's far too easy to slip from one month to the next. Instead, I like to talk in terms of quarters: there are four three-month quarters every year. Generally this gives you enough of a window that you'll almost always be able to deliver on time.

Next, you're going to have to talk about what you'll be delivering. First off, **let's talk about what you should not talk about**. Unless they are a big deal, don't talk about bug fixes, behind the scenes tweaks, or other changes that won't put new functionality in the hands of your customers. Instead, focus on the big functions and provide each one with a name and a brief description of what it will allow your customers to do.

Finally, you are going to want to make sure that when your customers look at their roadmap, **they realize that it only describes a point-in-time** – things will change. This means that you need to clearly label which version of the customer facing roadmap they are looking at. I like to put the quarter that the roadmap was made in the upper right hand corner: "3Q15". This means that if they pick up an old roadmap, they will quickly understand that it is out-of-date.

What Does All Of This Mean For You

In order to win new customers and to hang on to the customers that you already have for your product, our product manager job description tells us that a product manager needs to do a good job of **telling them about all of the wonderful new things that are going to be happening with his or her product**. A great way to go about doing this is to create a customer facing roadmap. These roadmaps can be a bit tricky to create correctly...

Every customer facing roadmap that you create **must contain just enough information to answer your customer's questions, but not so much information that it can be used against you when it falls into the hands of your competitors**. This means that you are going to have to pick a high-level timeframe to tell your customers when they will be receiving new functionality. Additionally, you are going to have include descriptions of only the most important functions at a very high level. Finally, add information to let your customers know what timeframe this roadmap covers and you will have completed this task.

A customer facing product roadmap is a part of every product manager's product development definition. As important as they are, **they can be tricky to do correctly**. Follow the rules that we've identified for you and you'll be able to create a roadmap that both meets the needs of your customers as well as your product. With a little luck your customer facing roadmap will cause more potential customers to turn into real customers!

Chapter 7

What Can Product Managers Learn From How The iPhone Was Born?

Chapter 7: What Can Product Managers Learn From How The iPhone Was Born?

If you are like most product managers, you look at the iPhone and **wish that it was the product that you were** managing. I mean, how cool would that be? Who wouldn't want to be in charge of a product that has sold over 470M copies? One of the things that we often overlook is that once upon a time the iPhone didn't exist. How it came into being is a story that holds some important lessons for product managers...

Keeping The Boss Happy

Steve Jobs is no longer with us, but everyone remembers him, right? Steve played a major role in the product development definition of [the iPhone](). He spent a great deal of his time **telling his development teams that he wanted bigger ideas and bigger concepts**.

One of the things that Steve insisted on during the development of the iPhone was **close communication with the team that was developing the product**. This meant that the team was required to make twice monthly presentations to Jobs in a conference room that had no windows. Clearly secrecy was an important part of this project!

What the product managers discovered is that every time they presented the product to someone else on the Apple senior management team, [Steve would step in and do more and more of the presentation](). Clearly he was in the process of **taking ownership of this product**.

Details, Details, Details

It can be hard to remember it today, but when the iPhone first came out **it really defined a new market – the smartphone**. What this meant is that a lot of the things that the iPhone did had never been done before. This meant that the product managers really had to spend a great deal of time focusing on the details of how the product worked. They knew that if they got this right, then it would be something that they could add to their product manager resume.

A great example of this is the iPhone's **"slide to unlock" feature**. This is one of the results of Apple's decision to do away with a physical keyboard and instead replace it with a touch screen keyboard. This had never been done before.

The attention to detail didn't stop there. The iPhone team was required to **revisit every detail about how mobile phones were being made** and reimagine them in order to understand how they could fit with the iPhone. This required revisiting things such as how to display a calendar and to how to check voice mail.

What All Of This Means For You

All product managers would like to be in charge of wildly successful products. One of the most successful products out there right now is the iPhone – who wouldn't want to be product managing that? What we forget is that just like every other product; the iPhone **had to be developed before it could be sold**. This fundamental fact is a part of every product manager job description.

Steve Jobs, the famous CEO, was **deeply involved in the design and creation of the iPhone**. The Apple product managers were not able to make their own decisions – Steve wanted to dictate how things were going to be down to the very last detail. The ultimate success of the iPhone came about because of the attention to detail that the phone's product managers had. There are lessons for all of us to learn from Apple's success with this product.

No, you and I may never be responsible for a product that will be as wildly popular as the iPhone is. However, that doesn't mean that we can't **learn from how the iPhone was developed**. What Apple did created a very successful product and that is something that we can all do.

Chapter 8

Applying Digital Product Management To Perfume

Chapter 8: Applying Digital Product Management To Perfume

Think, if you will, about the world of perfumes. This market consists of tiny little bottles that contain liquids that when sprayed on (most of the time) women produce scents that the wearer believes will make them more attractive to the opposite sex. Chanel No. 5 is considered to be the most expensive perfume in the world and is priced at $121.71 per ounce. Clearly there is a market for these scents; however, **can product managers bring the art of creating and selling perfume into the 21st Century?**

How Perfume Works Today

Ok, so let's say that you were a perfume product manager today. Just exactly **how would you be going about doing your job?** I must confess that since I am a guy, I am looking at this from the outside, but I think that I've been exposed to enough perfume advertising over the course of my life that I can take some educated guesses here.

New product development definition would take up a lot of your time. The "shelf life" of many perfume brands is relatively short – the world of perfume buying women is **always interested in what is new**, last year's fragrances hold no magic. If you are going to be developing new fragrances, then you are going have to be doing some research: what scents do women like? Sure you can do focus groups, but what may be even more telling is what scents are selling the best. This may be one reason why perfumes all seem to smell the same over time.

The next thing that you are going to have to do is to **market your product**. This is where things get really interesting. When you are picking a name for your new perfume, you are going to have to decide if you want the name to describe the scent or if you just want to make it sound mysterious and desirable. If you can get a celebrity to endorse your scent (think Britney Spears) then you will have created a perfume that everyone will want. Do this right and you'll have something to add to your product manager resume.

How Perfume Will Work Tomorrow

We are all now living in the 21st Century and so this means that even something as "old school" as marketing and selling perfume **can benefit from modern marketing tools**. What perfume product managers have come to realize is that there are simply too many scents out there for any one customer to have any chance of being to evaluate all of them. Clearly this is a problem that called for some help via technology.

That help has started to show up **via iPad apps and specialty algorithms**. The thinking here is that if some basic information can be collected from a woman regarding her likes and dislikes, the wide world of perfumes can be narrowed down to just those scents that will appeal to her.

One of the ways that these apps work is by having a woman **enter the names of the perfumes that she has liked in the past**. Once this information has been provided, then five different scents are provided. The customer is then asked to smell each as a part of a blind smell test so that they won't be influenced by packaging. Customers can also choose to "search by scent type" if they know what they like. Ultimately, the arrival of this new technology may fundamentally change how perfumes are designed and sold.

What All Of This Means For You

Perfume is a very interesting product. Clearly customers don't need it, they could get along just fine without it. However, at the same time it is very clear that **customers want it** – spraying on some perfume is a fundamental part of many women's toiletry every day. What this means for perfume product managers is that part of their product manager job description is that they have to guess what scents women want to buy.

Traditionally, stores have been stocked with all sorts of perfumes that advertised how they smelled by their name or how they were packaged. Women had to try on a large number of scents in order to find the one that worked the best with their skin chemistry. However, things are starting to change in the world of perfumes. Now **iPads and algorithms are being used to get answers from potential customers** in order to narrow down what types of scents will most likely appeal to them. With the large number of new scents that are introduced each year, keeping these apps and algorithms up-to-date can be a real challenge.

Perfume product managers need to be very careful. They are not selling industrial equipment that can be purchased sight unseen. Rather, they are creating and selling **a very personal product**. This means that they need to take the time to understand what scents women want to spray on themselves and then make sure that this is what they are providing.

Chapter 9

What Can ESPN Teach You About Growing Your Product?

Chapter 9: What Can ESPN Teach You About Growing Your Product?

If you like sports, then you like ESPN. ESPN is the dominate force in the world of broadcasting sports. In fact, they are so much a part of sports today that it's almost hard to remember a time when they didn't exist. However, there was a time that sports fans had to hunt in order to watch their favorite game. Somehow this all changed and now we instinctively go to ESPN in order to find out what is going on in the world of sports. **How did the ESPN product managers create a product development definition that allowed this to happen?**

What Makes ESPN Work?

That ESPN is a success is no big secret. However, how the ESPN product managers turned it into such a success is not quite so clear. As product managers, **this is the story that all of us would like to hear**. As you may have guessed, there is no one thing that they did that made them successful, but rather a number of different things.

One of the most important secrets to ESPN's success is the simple fact that it turns out that **it's a fun place to work**. Every member of the product team truly enjoys being there. Let's face it, sports are enjoyable. The people that ESPN hired played sports. What this meant was that they would then "play" the position that they were hired to fill. In one way, working at ESPN become a sort of the ultimate adult playground.

ESPN believes that its strategic advantage comes from the fact that it has been able to create a team-like environment within its workplace. This has led to workers who bring **a "never stop innovating" mentality** to the table. What ESPN does is to hire skilled people, place them on a team, and then let them do what they do best.

The Secret To ESPN's Success

One of ESPN's most successful shows is called **"Sports Center"**. During this nightly program, a recap of the day's events in sports is presented. This is not a new idea – it's been around for a long time. On these types of shows, they often focus on a single sport, show the highlights from that sport and then move on to the next sport.

What ESPN did that was so revolutionary was to **treat the show like it was a newspaper**. What this meant was that whatever was the lead story in sports would lead the broadcast off just like a headline. This could then be followed by the next story that might be about a completely different sport. When highlights were being presented from a game, they wouldn't be presented chronologically. Instead, they would be presented in order of their level of excitement. This kind of innovative thinking is what you want to have on your product manager resume.

It's important to note that **not everything that the ESPN product managers tried to do was a success**. Specifically, when they tried to open ESPN retail stores, no customers came. When they tried to create another sports channel, ESPN2, that was hipper than ESPN, that didn't go over very well either. However, they've learned from their mistakes and they've bounced back from them quickly.

What All Of This Means For You

When you ask almost anyone about televised sports, one of the first things that will pop into their head will be "ESPN". As product managers **we'd all like for our products to have that kind of brand appeal**. In fact, this is exactly what our product manager job description asks us to accomplish. However, we need to remember that things were not always this way. ESPN got to where they are today by the efforts of their product managers to promote the brand.

One of the most powerful things that ESPN has going for it occurs off-camera. They have created **a unique team-based work environment**. When staff join the company, they start to "play" their position. This has allowed a great deal of on-the-job innovation to occur. Another way that ESPN has risen to the top of the sports broadcasting world is via their popular Sports Center program. By copying the way that newspapers present information, they've created a unique and popular way to communicate the sports events of the day.

As product managers there are a number of different things that we can learn from how ESPN has become successful. We always need to remember that a product is not the result of one person's efforts, but rather what a team has been able to accomplish. Using the innovation that our product team can bring to the table is what will allow us to **create a product that can dominate our market and win the game** – just like ESPN!

Chapter 10

What Does The Internet Of Things Mean To Product Managers?

Chapter 10: What Does The Internet Of Things Mean To Product Managers?

Just in case you've been living with your head under a rock, there is this thing called **the "internet of things"** that is getting ready to take over the world. What is meant by the internet of things can vary from person to person, but basically what it means is the creation of a world in which everyday objects have network connectivity which then allows them to send and receive data. Things like refrigerators and washing machines. What's a product manager to do in order to get ready for a change like this?

The Internet Of Things Is All About Services

The interesting things about the internet of things is that there are a lot of product managers who are preparing for it to arrive before they update their product development definition. However, it turns out that it may already be here. There are product managers who believe that the internet of things is a collection of devices that have a chip in it that allows them to connect to the internet. However, the so-called killer app of the internet of things won't be a device, instead **it's going to be services**.

A great example of this is **the ride sharing service Uber**. In order for the Uber service to work correctly, the company needed to make its assets, drivers and cars, both smart and connected. They made this happen by providing each of their drivers with a smartphone app that allows them to fully automate the job of providing rides for people. This allows customers to purchase service (a ride) instead of having to worry about the technology that makes it possible. Uber product managers really have something to add to their product manager resume.

Another example of an internet of things service in action comes from **the Brita water filter company**. They have just introduced a new water filter that they are saying is part of the internet of things. When this water filter has used up its current filter, it has the ability to go online and order a new water filter to be delivered to your home. The thing to realize here is that the people who purchase this water filter are really buying a service (automatic reordering) and not a water filter.

Customers Really Don't Want Products, They Want Services

In the new era of the internet of things, what product managers are going to have to realize what customers are trying to do. What they want to accomplish is to solve problems that they have in their lives without having to worry about what technology is making this happen. What product managers are discovering is that when internet of things devices are considered to be a service by customers, then your customers **won't have to worry about how to get different devices to work together**.

Product managers who can focus on the service that they are offering to their customers are better able to clarify just exactly what they are offering. In some cases product managers are referring to what they are offering as being a **"hardware as a service"**. What this means is that because the company is making its money via subscription fees, when it comes time to upgrade the device, the company will take care of it. The customer won't be involved.

For customers of internet of things products, they really don't care about the underlying technology unless the product stops working. Product managers need to make sure that they don't get misled by the term internet of things. What they need to do is to spend their time asking why things should be connected.

Actually connecting them has become fairly easy, determining why they should be connected is the job of a product manager.

What All Of This Means For You

The arrival of the internet of things holds a great deal of promise and it also may [change the way that a lot of things are being done](). Product managers need to take the time to review their product manager job description and understand what this new technology really means and **how it will impact the products that they are responsible for**.

The internet of things has already arrived. It turns out that it's not really about devices that can be connected to the internet, instead **it's all about the services that can now be offered using those devices**. Uber has used the internet of things to connect its drivers with customers and Brita has used it to allow its water filters to order new filters when needed. Customers really don't care about the technology behind the internet of things, what they want is to use the devices to solve problems that are in their lives. Product managers need to spend their time understanding why different things should be connected to each other.

The internet of things has arrived. This opens a number of new product possibilities for product managers. What we need to realize is that what our customers are going to want is going to be the new services that they can get using internet enabled devices, not the devices themselves. If we can understand **what products would benefit from being connected to the internet**, then we'll have a successful product on our hands.

Chapter 11

Is Twitter Out Of Control?

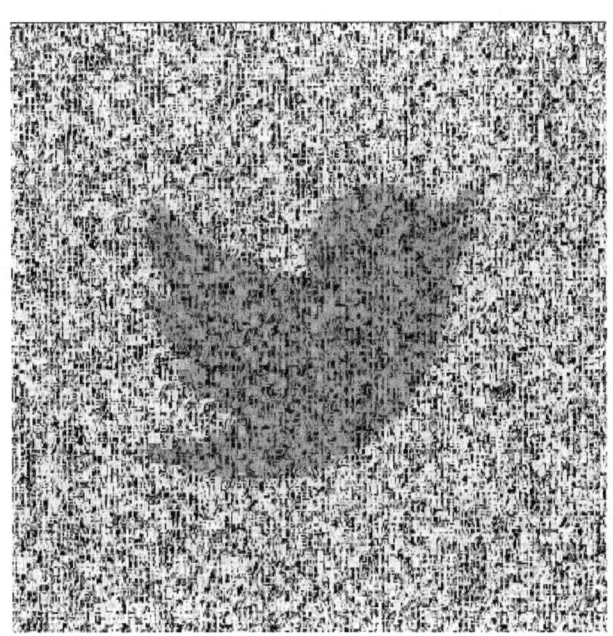

Chapter 11: Is Twitter Out Of Control?

Hopefully you are well aware of just who Twitter is. The micro blogging service has over 313 million monthly users (just think about adding that to your product manager resume). If you turn on just about any television program, they are always talking about what is being discussed on their Twitter feed. This is all very impressive, but a bigger question that the Twitter product managers have to answer is **just how many people are seeing all of those tweets?** The answer is that they don't know.

A Loss Of Control

So what's going on over at Twitter? We all know that Twitter is very, very popular. How many causes / ads / companies have you seen lately that are promoting a hashtag of some sort that they'd like you to start using on Twitter? What all of this attention means is that there are a great number of people who are using Twitter. However, that's where Twitter's problems with their product development definition start to show up. It turns out that **Twitter's content is reaching a lot more people than actually have Twitter accounts or who engage with Twitter on a daily basis**. The Twitter product managers have no way to count these people.

Twitter does try to measure the reach of its service. The Twitter product managers believe that the total reachable market for Twitter is 880 million people. This number includes people who are exposed to Twitter information outside of the main Twitter webpage and mobile applications. This can happen when people see Twitter information embedded in a website or a particular news article. There is no way to include all of the television shows where the hosts comment on and read off twitter messages.

What we need to understand here is that **the Twitter product managers have a massive problem on their hands**. Twitter likes to brag about its influence, but the problem is that they really don't know how many people they are reaching. The reason for this is that a great deal of the content that is on Twitter is being consumed outside of Twitter's applications so they have no way to measure it. Twitter does have valuable content, but because they do such a bad job of bringing it to the surface, an entire industry has sprung up to provide apps and data mining services.

What Twitter Needs To Do

The Twitter product managers are dealing with a fundamental problem here. Their company is very popular, but it is struggling. Twitter has not yet turned a profit and they recently reported that their growth in new membership in the past quarter was just 1%. The problem that Twitter is facing is the same problem that just about all media companies are currently facing. They do a great job of creating content that people want to see. However, **they are losing control over how people consume their content**.

The good news is that Twitter's product managers are taking steps to try to solve their problem. They have **implemented a new algorithm** that organizes the tweets that a user is looking at. The problem with what the product managers are doing is that the incremental changes that they are making simply are not enough. The problem is that Twitter contains a great deal of very valuable information that its users just can't access quick enough.

This need to change how things are done has placed the Twitter product managers in a classic situation. What they need to accomplish is to radically change how their service operates in order to gain new customers while at the same time not alienating those people who currently use the service. Perhaps

Twitter's biggest problem is that all of its tools are built to both create and capture content. Since so many people just want to read content and not create it, perhaps it's time for Twitter to **divide these functions up** and accept the fact that the majority of their content is created by a minority of their users.

What All Of This Means For You

Twitter is an amazingly popular service. A great number of people have signed up to use Twitter. **These people produce a great deal of content each day**. What is even more amazing is that more people than just that large group of people who have signed up read Twitter content each day. This is where Twitter is running into a problem and the Twitter product managers are going to have to consult their product manager job description to find out what they need to do.

The twitter product managers know how many users they have. They even know how many active users they have. However, **what they don't know is how many people are consuming Twitter content every day**. The reason that they don't know this is because a great deal of the consumption of the Twitter data is happening outside of twitter's applications so they have no way to track it. Twitter creates great content, but they have no way to track how it's being consumed. The product managers are taking steps to try to create tools that will do a better job of providing users with the information that they want, but it may be too little too late. What Twitter needs to do is to separate the tools for consuming content from the tools for creating content.

Twitter is a very good service that is used by a very large group of people. Now all their product managers need to do is to determine how to **make all of their great content available to the people who want to consume it**. If they aren't careful, outside firms will end up doing this better than they can. Let's hope that the Twitter product managers get the message!

Chapter 12

Amazon Plans On Getting Into The Grocery Business

Chapter 12: Amazon Plans On Getting Into The Grocery Business

Hopefully by now we are all aware that Amazon has purchased Whole Foods and has **gotten into the grocery business in a big way**. However, what a lot of product managers may not be aware of is that Amazon's grocery dreams don't stop with Whole Foods. Instead, they have their own plans about changing their product development definition and finding out what an Amazon grocery store that they built from the ground up would look like. What lessors are product managers going to be able to learn as we watch Amazon expand even further into the grocery business?

Amazon's Plans For The Grocery Business

We all know that Amazon has been very, very successful in the business of selling books, DVDs, etc. However, just exactly how do they plan on going about getting into the world of **selling groceries** if they have to build their own stores? The word on the street is that Amazon is planning on introducing a new type of grocery store. This store will act like a convenience store. It also plans on offering curb side pickup service. The plan is to create small brick-and-mortar stores that will offer produce, meats, milk, and other perishable items that customers can pick up and take home.

Amazon wants to make the process of finding the grocery items that you want quick, easy, and modern. That's why they are planning on allowing their customers to **use their mobile phones to select the items that they want**. If a customer chooses to not use their phone, then the thinking is that they can use the touchscreen systems that will be installed in every store to pick out the items that they are looking for. The plan is to allow customers to also be able to order items that have a longer shelf life and be able to have same day delivery of these items.

Amazon understands that for many of their customers, time is a precious thing. What this means is that Amazon plans on offering **designated drive-in locations** where online grocery shoppers will have the groceries that they have ordered brought out to their car Just to make things even faster, Amazon is planning on using license plate reading technology to help speed up the lines at these locations. Initially, the only people who will be able to shop at Amazon's grocery stores will be the people who are currently members of Amazon's Fresh subscription service. Currently this service provides same day delivery of food at set times. If you are already an Amazon Prime member, you can subscribe to the Fresh service for $15 / month.

How Amazon Plans On Being Successful

What Amazon seems to be thinking is that people really don't want to have to go to the effort of scheduling a trip to the grocery store, going, wandering up and down aisles searching for that they need, and then lugging it all home. Who has the time for all that? Instead, **Amazon believes that we simply want to pick up the food that we need on our way home from work**. The Amazon product managers are going to be competing with the grocery discounters and, of course, with Walmart. Walmart has recently announced that they will expanding the number of locations where they plan on offering pick up service for groceries.

So how big is this market? Right now groceries account for about 20% of the average consumers spending. Online purchases of groceries currently only account for 2% of U.S. grocery store sales. The people who study such things think that the online grocery market **could double to over US$42B this year**. Going after that market would look good on anyone's product manager resume. Right now 8% of people say that they get their groceries delivered to them. However, 26% expect to do it this year.

The reason that the Amazon product managers are so interested in getting into the grocery market is because consumers restock their refrigerator each week. What this means is that Amazon will have more opportunities to sell more profitable items along with staples like milk. Americans average 1.5 visits to the grocery store each week. They tend to spend $107. This means that they spend a total of $5,500 per year. This is double the $2,500 that Amazon Prime members tend to spend with Amazon and 10x the amount that non-Prime members spend. Amazon is very aware of the dot.com firms such as Webvan that have tried this in the past and failed. Amazon is taking it slow and hopes to be successful.

What All Of This Means For You

Amazon is a very large and successful company. However, its product managers have looked at their product manager job description and realized that in order for the company to remain successful they are going to have to **find and conquer new markets**. This is why Amazon is in the process of exploring how best to enter the grocery business. Even though they have purchased Whole Foods, they still want to try to build their own unique grocery stores from the ground up.

Amazon wants to create a new type of grocery store that acts like a convenience store. These stores will allow consumers to order on their mobile phones and pick up using curb side service. The stores will offer items with short shelf lives like milk and meat. Items with longer shelf lives can be delivered directly to a customer's home. Amazon understands that time is critical to their potential customers. That's why they are trying to make the grocery shopping experience as quick and painless as possible. By entering into this space, Amazon is going to be competing directly with Walmart. This is a very large market and people visit the grocery store more than one time a week. This means that Amazon can start to sell more costly items. Consumers spend a lot on groceries each year and Amazon wants to capture a portion of that.

The grocery business is a tough business to be in. Home delivery can be challenging and costly. However, Amazon has deep pockets and if any company can do this, then they are probably the ones who can pull it off. Amazon is going to **have to be very patient** and take the time to really learn what their customers want from a grocery store

It's from the forge of failure that the steel of success is formed.

Hard Work Does Not Guarantee Success, But Success Does Not Happen Without Hard Work.

- Dr. Jim Anderson

Create Products Your Customers Want At A Price That They Are Willing To Pay!

Dr. Jim Anderson is available to provide training and coaching on the two topics that are the most important to product managers everywhere: how do I create the products that my customers want and what should I price them at?

Dr. Anderson believes that in order to both learn and remember what he says, product managers need to laugh. Each one of his speeches is full of fun and humor so that what he says "sticks" with everyone.

Dr. Anderson's Product Management Training Includes:

1. How can you segment your market?
2. What problems are your customers having right now?
3. Which of your customer's problems does your product solve?
4. How much of this problem does your product solve?
5. How much will it cost your customer if they don't fix this problem?

Dr. Jim Anderson presents over 100 speeches per year. To invite Dr. Anderson to speak at your event, contact him at:

Phone: 813-418-6970 or
Email: jim@BlueElephantConsulting.com

Photo Credits:

Cover - Hembo Pagi

https://www.flickr.com/photos/hembo/

Chapter 1 - Pictures of Money

https://www.flickr.com/photos/pictures-of-money/

Chapter 2 - Veronica Foale

https://www.flickr.com/photos/sleeplessnights/3399921783/

Chapter 3 - Filip Lachowski

https://www.flickr.com/photos/malczyk/5638599313/

Chapter 4 - Guy Kilroy

https://www.flickr.com/photos/124808053@N07/

Chapter 5 - William Warby

https://www.flickr.com/photos/wwarby/

Chapter 6 - Judy McCallum

https://www.flickr.com/photos/joodmc/

Chapter 7 - Miki Uchida

https://www.flickr.com/photos/mk_7500/

Chapter 8 - Kevin Jaako

https://www.flickr.com/photos/jaako/

Chapter 9 - Matt Dempsey

https://www.flickr.com/photos/matt44053/

Chapter 10 - Philip McMaster

https://www.flickr.com/photos/dragonpreneur/

Chapter 11 - Esther Vargas

https://www.flickr.com/photos/esthervargasc/

Chapter 12 - Francis Chang

https://www.flickr.com/photos/minutedreamer/

Other Books By The Author

Product Management

- How Product Managers Can Sell More Of Their Product: Tips & Techniques For Product Managers To Better Understand How To Sell Their Product

- How Product Managers Can Sell More Of Their Product: Tips & Techniques For Product Managers To Better Understand How To Sell Their Product

- How To Create A Successful Product That Customers Will Want: Techniques For Product Managers To Boost Product Sales And Increase Customer Satisfaction

- What Product Managers Need To Know About World-Class Product Development: How Product Managers Can Create Successful Products

- How Product Managers Can Learn To Understand Their Customers: Techniques For Product Managers To Better Understand What Their Customers Really Want

- Product Management Secrets: Techniques For Product Managers To Boost Product Sales And Increase Customer Satisfaction

- Product Development Lessons For Product Managers: How Product Managers Can Create Successful Products

- Customer Lessons For Product Managers: Techniques For Product Managers To Better Understand What Their Customers Really Want

- Product Failure Lessons For Product Managers: Examples Of Products That Have Failed For Product Managers To Learn From

- Communication Skills For Product Managers: The Communication Skills That Product Managers Need To Know How To Use In Order To Have A Successful Product

- How To Have A Successful Product Manager Career: The Things That You Need To Be Doing TODAY In Order To Have A Successful Product Manager Career

- Product Manager Product Success: How to keep your product on track and make it become a success

Public Speaking

- Creating Speeches That Work: How To Create A Speech That Will Make Your Message Be Remembered Forever!

- How To Organize A Speech In Order To Make Your Point: How to put together a speech that will capture and hold your audience's attention

- Changing How You Speak To Overcome Your Fear Of Speaking: Change techniques that will transform a speech into a memorable event

- Delivering Excellence: How To Give Presentations That Make A Difference: Presentation techniques that will transform a speech into a memorable event

- Tools Speakers Need In Order To Give The Perfect Speech: What tools to use to create your next speech so that your message will be remembered forever!

- How To Create A Speech That Will Be Remembered

- Secrets To Organizing A Speech For Maximum Impact: How to put together a speech that will capture and hold your audience's attention

- How To Become A Better Speaker By Changing How You Speak: Change techniques that will transform a speech into a memorable event

- How To Give A Great Presentation: Presentation techniques that will transform a speech into a memorable event

- How To Rehearse In Order To Give The Perfect Speech: How to effectively rehearse your next speech to that your message be remembered forever!

- Secrets To Creating The Perfect Speech: How to create a speech that will make your message be remembered forever!

- Secrets To Organizing The Perfect Speech: How to organize the best speech of your life!

- Secrets To Planning The Perfect Speech: How to plan to give the best speech of your life

- How To Show What You Mean During A Presentation: How to use visual techniques to transform a speech into a memorable event

- **CIO Skills**

- How CIOs Can Bring Business And IT Together: How CIOs Can Use Their Technical Skills To Help Their Company Solve Real-World Business Problems

- New IT Technology Issues Facing CIOs: How CIOs Can Stay On Top Of The Changes In The Technology That Powers The Company

- Keeping The Barbarians Out: How CIOs Can Secure Their Department and Company: Tips And Techniques For CIOs To Use In Order To Secure Both Their IT Department And Their Company

- What CIOs Need To Know In Order To Successfully Manage An IT Department: Decision Making Skills That Every CIO Needs To Have In Order To Be Able To Make The Right Choices

- Becoming A Powerful And Effective Leader: Tips And Techniques That IT Managers Can Use In Order To Develop Leadership Skills

- CIO Secrets For Growing Innovation: Tips And Techniques For CIOs To Use In Order To Make Innovation Happen In Their IT Department

- Your Success As A CIO Depends On How Well You Communicate: Tips And Techniques For CIOs To

Use In Order To Become Better Communicators

- What CIOs Need To Know About Working With Partners: Techniques For CIOs To Use In Order To Be Able To Successfully Work With Partners

- Critical CIO Management Skills: Decision Making Skills That Every CIO Needs To Have In Order To Be Able To Make The Right Choices

- How CIOs Can Make Innovation Happen: Tips And Techniques For CIOs To Use In Order To Make Innovation Happen In Their IT Department

- CIO Communication Skills Secrets: Tips And Techniques For CIOs To Use In Order To Become Better Communicators

- Managing Your CIO Career: Steps That CIOs Have To Take In Order To Have A Long And Successful Career

- CIO Business Skills: How CIOs can work effectively with the rest of the company!

- **IT Manager Skills**

- How IT Managers Can Use New Technology To Meet Today's IT Challenges: Technologies That IT Managers Can Use In Order to Make Their Teams

More Productive

- How To Build High Performance IT Teams: Tips And Techniques That IT Managers Can Use In Order To Develop Productive Teams

- Save Yourself, Save Your Job – How To Manage Your IT Career: Secrets That IT Managers Can Use In Order To Have A Successful Career

- Growing Your CIO Career: How CIOs Can Work With The Entire Company In Order To Be Successful

- How IT Managers Can Make Innovation Happen: Tips And Techniques For IT Managers To Use In Order To Make Innovation Happen In Their Teams

- Staffing Skills IT Managers Must Have: Tips And Techniques That IT Managers Can Use In Order To Correctly Staff Their Teams

- Secrets Of Effective Leadership For IT Managers: Tips And Techniques That IT Managers Can Use In Order To Develop Leadership Skills

- IT Manager Career Secrets: Tips And Techniques That IT Managers Can Use In Order To Have A Successful Career

- IT Manager Budgeting Skills: How IT Managers Can Request, Manage, Use, And Track Their Funding

- Secrets Of Managing Budgets: What IT Managers Need To Know In Order To Understand How Their Company Uses Money

<u>Negotiating</u>

- The Art Of Packaging A Negotiation: How To Develop The Skill Of Assembling Potential Trades In Order To Get The Best Possible Outcome

- Getting What You Want In A Negotiation By Learning How To Signal: How To Develop The Skill Of Effective Signaling In A Negotiation In Order To Get The Best Possible Outcome

- Exploring How To Get The Deal That You Want In A Negotiation: How To Develop The Skill Of Exploring What Is Possible In A Negotiation In Order To Reach The Best Possible Deal

- Use The Power Of Arguing To Win Your Next Negotiation: How To Develop The Skill Of Effective Arguing In A Negotiation In Order To Get The Best Possible Outcome

- Learn How To Signal In Your Next Negotiation: How To Develop The Skill Of Effective Signaling In A

Negotiation In Order To Get The Best Possible Outcome

- Learn The Skill Of Exploring In A Negotiation: How To Develop The Skill Of Exploring What Is Possible In A Negotiation In Order To Reach The Best Possible Deal

- Learn How To Argue In Your Next Negotiation: How To Develop The Skill Of Effective Arguing In A Negotiation In Order To Get The Best Possible Outcome|

- How To Open Your Next Negotiation: How To Start A Negotiation In Order To Get The Best Possible Outcome

- Preparing For Your Next Negotiation: What You Need To Do BEFORE A Negotiation Starts In Order To Get The Best Possible Deal

- Learn How To Package Trades In Your Next Negotiation

- All Good Things Come To An End: How To Close A Negotiation - How To Develop The Skill Of Closing In Order To Get The Best Possible Outcome From A Negotiation

- Take No Prisoners In Your Next Negotiation: How To Start A Negotiation In Order To Get The Best Possible Outcome

Miscellaneous

- How To Heal A Broken Leg – Fast!: Understanding how to deal with a broken leg in order to start walking again quickly

- How Software Defined Networking (SDN) Is Going To Change Your World Forever: The Revolution In Network Design And How It Affects You

- The Power Of Virtualization: How It Affects Memory, Servers, and Storage: The Revolution In Creating Virtual Devices And How It Affects You

- The Internet-Enabled Successful School District Superintendent: How To Use The Internet To Boost Parental Involvement In Your Schools

- Power Distribution Unit (PDU) Secrets: What Everyone Who Works In A Data Center Needs To Know!

- Making The Jump: How To Land Your Dream Job When You Get Out Of College!

- How To Use The Internet To Create Successful Students And Involved Parents

Techniques For Product Managers To Better Understand What Their Customers Really Want

> This book has been written with one goal in mind – to show you how to find out what your customers really want from your product. We're going to show you how to listen to what your customers are really telling you.
>
> **Let's Make Your Product A Success!**

What You'll Find Inside:

- **PRODUCT MANAGERS NEED TO KNOW WHAT THEIR COMPANY'S COST OF CAPITAL IS**

- **THE SECRET TO CREATING A CUSTOMER-FACING PRODUCT ROADMAP**

- **HOW TO CREATE A PRODUCT TIMELINE THAT WORKS**

- **WHAT DOES THE INTERNET OF THINGS MEAN TO PRODUCT MANAGERS?**

Dr. Jim Anderson brings his 4 college degrees coupled with over 25 years of real-world experience to this book. He's managed products at some of the world's largest firms as well as at start-ups. He's going to show you what you need to do in order to make your career a success!

www.ingramcontent.com/pod-product-compliance
Lightning Source LLC
Chambersburg PA
CBHW070206230526
45471CB00002B/838